KALEIDOSCOPE COLLECTION

Josiah's Jacket

Reva Lobatos

Illustrated by Chao Tsai

Consulting Editor
Joy Cowley

"Let's go to the park,"
Dad said to Josiah.
"Put on your new jacket."

Josiah and Dad went to the park.
Josiah had fun on the slide.

He went on the swing,
and Dad pushed him.

Josiah went around and around. "Look at me!" he called to Dad.

On the way home,
Josiah looked at his jacket.
One of the buttons was missing!

Josiah cried and cried.
"My jacket is not good now!"

Mom brought out her button jar. "I will sew on a new button," she said to Josiah.

Mom tipped the buttons onto the floor.
"Choose a button," she said.

There were big buttons
and little buttons—
buttons of every color.

"I want this yellow button," Josiah said to Mom. "Please sew it on my jacket."

"I love it!" Josiah shouted.
"No one has a jacket like mine!"

The next day,
Josiah ran into the house.
He was very excited.

"Look! Look!" he shouted.
"I lost another button!"